EARTHWISE

Ecosystems

Jim Pipe

Franklin Watts
London • Sydney

CONTENTS

© Aladdin Books Ltd 2004

Designed and produced by
Aladdin Books Ltd
2-3 Fitzroy Mews
London W1T 6DF

ISBN 0 7496 5497 X

Reprinted in Malaysia 2005

First published in
Great Britain in 2004 by
Franklin Watts
338 Euston Road
London NW1 3BH

Franklin Watts Australia
Hachette Children's Books
Level 17/207 Kent Street
Sydney NSW 2000

A catalogue record for this
book is available from the
British Library.

Design
Flick, Book Design and
Graphics

Editor
Katie Harker

Educational Consultant
Jackie Holderness

Picture Research
Brian Hunter Smart

INTRODUCTION

Whether you are in the garden, out for a walk or swimming in the sea, there is an incredible world of wildlife all around you.

This book looks at how plants, animals and people live with and affect each other. It also shows what you can do to help the wildlife in your area.

HOW TO USE THIS BOOK

Look for the symbol of the magnifying glass for tips on how to observe wildlife in your local area.

The paintbrush boxes contain a wildlife activity or project that you can try yourself.

ANIMAL HOMES

You can find plants and animals just about everywhere. They live in ponds, woods and hedges, even in old walls and rubbish dumps. These places are all habitats. Habitats are homes that provide living things with the food, water and shelter they need. Next time you lift up a big stone, see what lives in the habitat underneath it!

EXPLORE!

Why not take a look at habitats, such as streams, meadows and woods, near your house or school? There are lots of animals and plants to spot up in the air, on the ground and underwater! Always ask an adult to walk around with you, and be especially careful near water. Water can be dangerous, even for good swimmers!

Habitats Big and Small
Smaller habitats are part of bigger habitats. A patch of grass can be a small habitat on its own, but it may be in a wood. The wood is a larger habitat that is home to a wider group of animals, such as deer and squirrels.

Wildlife Scenes

What plants or animals do you like to paint? Some artists make their wildlife scenes look as real as possible. Other artists capture the mood of a scene, as in *White Horse* by Paul Gauguin (left). Try this yourself – paint a wildlife scene in different ways to create different moods.

Animal, Vegetable and Mineral!

Habitats are made up of living and non-living things. A pond habitat (above) includes the air that animals breathe, the water they swim in, the plants growing in the pond, and rocks and mud at the bottom of the pond.

City Homes

Many plants and animals have learned to survive in towns. Birds (above) make their nests on tall buildings. Rubbish dumps are a good habitat for rats. Other town habitats are riverbanks and parks.

COMMUNITY LIVING

Every habitat is home to a group of plants and animals, called a community. Together, a habitat and its community are known as an ecosystem. For example, a tree is a simple ecosystem. Its community is made up of the birds, insects, snails, moss and fungi that live on it.

Food Chain

All the living things in an ecosystem depend on each other for food. In any ecosystem, plants use the Sun's energy and water to make food. This energy is passed onto plant-eating animals, which are eaten by meat-eating animals, called predators.

Food chains (right) are a way of showing how a series of organisms are linked together in their feeding habits. The smallest organism is typically eaten by a larger one, which in turn is eaten by an even larger organism.

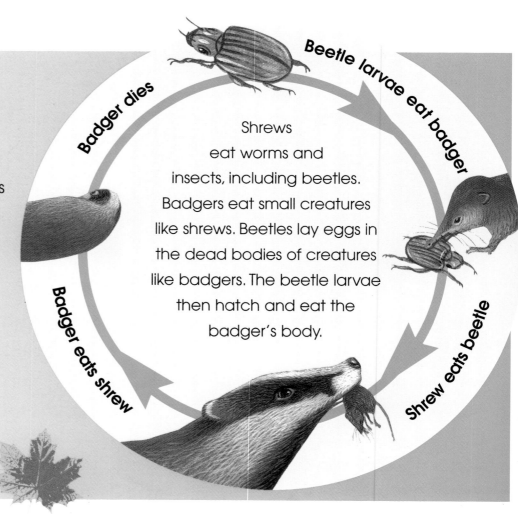

Shrews eat worms and insects, including beetles. Badgers eat small creatures like shrews. Beetles lay eggs in the dead bodies of creatures like badgers. The beetle larvae then hatch and eat the badger's body.

Badger dies

Beetle larvae eat badger

Shrew eats beetle

Badger eats shrew

OLD • WALL

If you look closely, you will be amazed by the number of animals and plants living in an old wall. Plants use runners and suckers to cling to the wall. Bricks and bushes provide shelter for mice, lizards and birds. Snails, wasps and ants live in cracks in the wall. Slugs and woodlice live in damp areas below the wall.

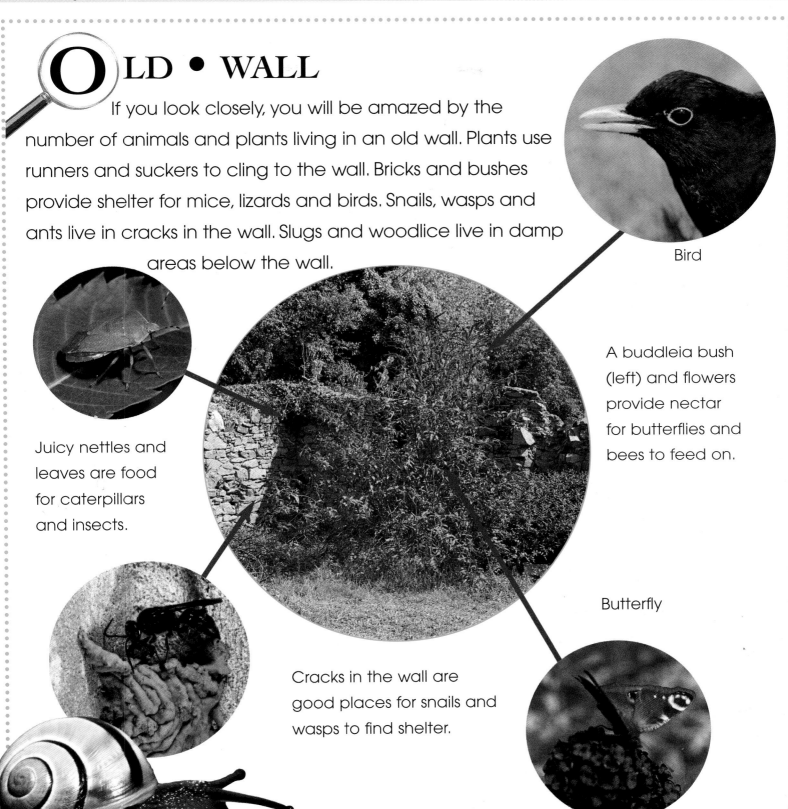

Bird

A buddleia bush (left) and flowers provide nectar for butterflies and bees to feed on.

Juicy nettles and leaves are food for caterpillars and insects.

Butterfly

Cracks in the wall are good places for snails and wasps to find shelter.

PONDS AND LAKES

Some of the most interesting ecosystems in your local area are ponds and lakes. The water in lakes and ponds is usually still, so there are often more plants than in fast-flowing rivers and streams. Animals in the pond need each other, especially at dinner time! Tiny creatures that feed on plants are eaten by insects, such as dragonflies. Insects are then eaten by frogs and fish who are food for larger fish and birds.

You can use binoculars to watch pond wildlife.

Bird Watching

Lakes are a good place to watch birds, such as this heron. It has a long, thin beak to spear fish and long legs to wade in deep water.

Find some cover, get comfortable, keep still and quiet, and be patient! Write down details of the birds you do not know, such as their colours, markings and shape. Then look them up in a book about birds when you get home.

Herons usually nest in trees near water.

P OND • **LIFE**

Look for wildlife in and around your local pond. Water plants live under the surface of ponds and lakes. Some plants are attached to the bottom, while others float free. The plants provide food and shelter for creatures such as water insects, snails, frogs and fish.

See if you can spot dragonflies whizzing through the air, ducklings on the surface or frogs poking their heads out of the water. If you visit a lake or pond, always take an adult with you – water can be dangerous.

Dragonfly

Ducks

Many country ponds have been drained in the last 50 years, so there are fewer habitats for pond creatures than before. Other ponds near cities and factories have become so dirty and polluted (right) that animals can't live there anymore. As a result, garden ponds are now an important home for newts, frogs, toads and birds.

WOODS AND FORESTS

Every tree in a forest is a home for wildlife. Deciduous trees, like oak and apple, have wide flat leaves that fall in autumn. They also provide nuts or fruit for animals to eat. The forest floor is covered in a thick layer of dying plant and animal matter, called humus. This is broken down by worms and insects, which are food for bigger animals.

Plant a Tree

You can create a future habitat by planting a young tree, called a sapling. Dig a hole as wide as the roots and just deep enough for them to sit in. Place the tree carefully in the hole. Then shovel in some soil and push or tread it down gently (right). Keep doing this until the hole is filled. Water your tree daily.

FOREST • **L**IFE

A forest is full of wildlife. As well as forest flowers, such as foxgloves, look out for mosses, ferns and mushrooms. Under the leaves you may find beetles and centipedes, as well as fallen nuts and berries. Up in the trees, watch for squirrels or birds such as crows, jays and blackbirds, or even a sleeping owl!

Owl

Squirrel

Centipede

Shellfish can be seen as the tide goes out.

SEASHORE

The tide and the slope of a beach create different habitats along a seashore where wildlife can live. On a cliff face, flowers and bushes grow and seabirds nest. At the bottom of the cliff are boulders and stones from landslides. Nearer the sea are rock pools, pebbles or sand.

Collecting Shells

The empty shells you find on a beach were once home to molluscs, such as snails, clams and oysters. Molluscs are animals with soft bodies that have no skeleton. Crustaceans, like crabs, also leave shells behind. Using books or the internet, can you find out the names of these creatures?

Hermit crab

Pollution is a major problem for seashore habitats. Oil spills can damage wide stretches of coastline. Storms at sea carry floating rubbish from towns and ships onto beaches. This rubbish is known as flotsam. It can include ropes, bottles and even containers holding dangerous chemicals. Rubbish is a danger to sea animals. A plastic bag can kill a turtle. Turtles swallow the bags because they look like jellyfish.

Rock • Pools

Rock pools are left behind when the tide goes out. They are interesting habitats to explore, but remember to wear shoes that won't slip easily. If you are lucky, you may find sea anemones, barnacles, crabs, sea urchins, starfish, seaweeds, shrimps and small fish. When you are looking, remember that most of the animals that live in rock pools cannot survive out of water. Also, always replace rocks that you move. They are probably an animal's home!

Always tell an adult where you are exploring!

Starfish

Crab

Sea anemone

BIOMES

A rockpool on a beach is a small ecosystem on a bigger one. Lakes, woods, seashores and even whole countries can be grouped together in giant ecosystems called biomes. Each biome is affected by its weather and climate. The wildlife in the biome will depend on how hot or wet it is in that part of the world.

WOOD • WISE

You can help ecosystems on the other side of the world! If you buy wood or paper products with the Forest Stewardship Council (FSC) logo, you can be sure that they come from trees in forests where rare trees are protected.

The FSC sets standards that ensure that forestry is practised in an environmentally responsible way.

FSC

Dry grasslands
- hot summers, cold winters
- grassy plains
- antelope, buffalo

Biomes around the world

This map shows where biomes are found around the world. Most biomes are named after the main kind of plant found in it. Each biome is home to a large variety of plants and animals.

Mountains
- cold and wet
- conifer trees
- goats, small mammals

Savanna
- hot all year, wet and dry seasons
- grassland and trees
- lions, elephants

Tropical rainforests
(see page 16-17)
- hot and very wet
- millions of different plants and animals

Deciduous forests
(see page 10)
- warm summers, cold winters
- deer, squirrels, birds

Coniferous forests
(see page 10)
- very cold winters
- bears, raccoons

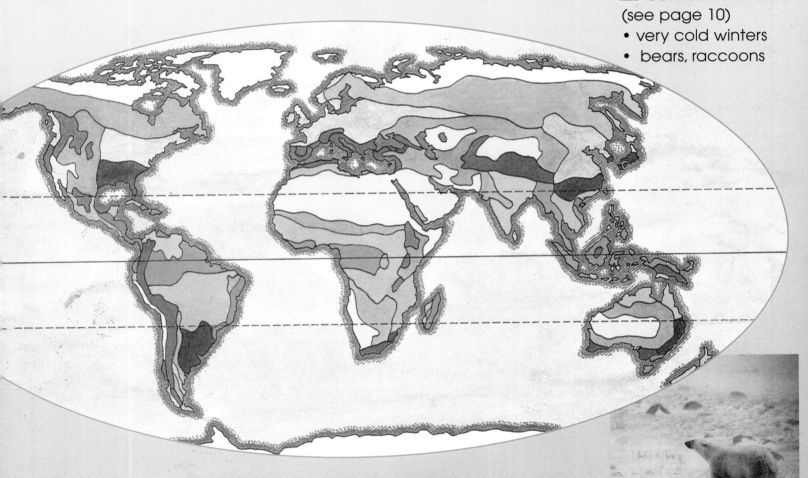

Deserts
(see page 18)
- very hot and dry
- few plants
- lizards, snakes and small mammals

Scrubland
- warm wet winters, hot, dry summers
- shrubs with hard leaves
- coyotes, lizards

Subtropical forest
(see page 16-17)
- warm or cold depending on region
- millions of different plants and animals

Polar regions
- very cold and dry
- almost no plants
- polar bears, seals

RAINFORESTS

Half of the rainforests have already been destroyed. The forests are still being cut down and cleared at an incredible speed. Forest fires in Indonesia (above) and Brazil have also destroyed huge areas of forest.

One of the most exciting habitats are the rainforests. They are found near to the equator, in countries such as Brazil and Indonesia. Here, it is hot and rainy all year round, helping giant trees and many other plants to grow. The forests are also home to millions of animals, such as birds, snakes and monkeys.

FOREST • FRUITS

Rainforests contain over half of all the known wildlife on the planet. Forest plants are a vital source of raw materials for medicines and foods, and they help to create the oxygen that animals breathe. Wood from forest trees is used in furniture and buildings. Bananas, peanuts, coconuts, rubber, house plants and the cacao beans used in chocolate all come from the world's rainforests. We need to find a way to make use of these resources without destroying the forests.

Chocolate

Bananas

Rainforests are made up of layers. Different groups of plants and animals live on the forest floor, in the branches or in the treetops.

Forest Safari

Write a story about a trip through the rainforest. Rivers are the roads of the rainforest, so you could travel by canoe, then walk through the hot, steamy jungle. Imagine the amazing animals you might see, such as jaguars, tree frogs, crocodiles and giant spiders, and think of the noises they make!

Scarlet macaws, jaguars and tree frogs are all found in the tropical forests of South America.

DESERTS

Compared to a rainforest, a desert is a very tough habitat to live in. Deserts are the driest places in the world and, without rain, few plants can survive in the sandy or rocky soil. Desert plants and animals, such as rabbits, foxes, snakes and lizards, have special bodies that help them to store water or keep cool.

Yellow-breasted chat

There is water in the ground under a desert. If this water reaches the surface, it makes a pool or "oasis". Trees and other plants grow around the pool. For short periods, even deserts are full of life. The seeds wait until there is enough water for them to grow. After a rainstorm, the desert is covered with flowers.

Cactus spines protect the plant from hungry animals and act as a windbreak to prevent dehydration from dry winds.

Many animals have found different ways to survive in the desert. Some animals only come out in the cool of the night. Desert lizards move quickly over hot surfaces, stopping only in shady places. Many desert animals are pale in colour to absorb less heat and to keep them camouflaged.

A gila monster stores valuable fat in its tail. It can survive on this fat for three months.

This jackrabbit has big ears to help it hunt at night. They also help to keep it cool during the day!

In a sandy desert, the wind heaps the sand into hills called dunes.

Desert Garden

Cacti are some of the most exciting and exotic houseplants you can look after. A container filled with sandy soil and stones is all you need to grow your own cactus garden. Once you have planted your cacti, they will need very little water as they store it in their thick stems. But they love lots of sunshine, so put them in a sunny place!

OCEANS

When you go for a swim in the sea, you are part of a very large ecosystem – the oceans. In the oceans you can find many different habitats, such as the spectacular coral reefs found in warm waters. Most ocean life exists in the top 100 metres of water, where there is some sunlight. Below, in the dark waters of the deep, some very weird and wonderful creatures live.

Lobster

Sea creatures, such as fish, squid and crabs, are an important food source for human beings. But many kinds, or species, of fish and turtles (left) are in danger because modern fishing boats drag long nets through the water. These give the animals no chance to escape. In the Atlantic Ocean, numbers of herring, haddock and cod are very low. Many species of dolphin and whale are also under threat.

All sea creatures depend on plants for food. The most important marine plants, called phytoplankton, are so small they can only be seen with a microscope. These are eaten by tiny animals called zooplankton. These are eaten by small fish that are food for larger fish. Amazingly, 30-metre blue whales also feed on zooplankton called krill (right). The whales eat over 60 million krill per day.

S EA • CATCH

Many other resources come from the ocean. A giant seaweed, called kelp, is used in making ice cream, salad dressing and make-up! Clay found in the sea is rich in minerals and often used for beauty products. Sea salt is used as a flavouring in food. Look out for other ocean products, such as natural sponges, coral, the pearls and shells used in jewellery and medicines made from sea animals.

THREAT TO HABITATS

People are destroying habitats all over the world. As cities grow larger or more land is cleared for farms, there is less room for wildlife. Pollution has poisoned many European forests. Global warming, the result of overheating of the atmosphere, is destroying coral reefs in the oceans. The activities of human beings are changing the world's climate so fast that some plants and animals are struggling to survive.

By destroying the rainforests we risk losing many plants that might one day cure serious illnesses.

DEVELOPMENTS

Perhaps you have noticed changes in your area where woods or meadows are being replaced by buildings or roads? When natural habitats like these disappear, so do the wild plants and animals that depend on them. Clearing the rainforests has forced millions of forest people out of their homes.

Deforestation in your area may be affecting plants and animals too.

When a habitat is destroyed, plants, animals and people all lose out. Scientists fear that half of the world's wildlife could disappear in the next 50 years.

People also depend on healthy habitats for food and fresh water. Many medicines (above) and herbal remedies also come from rare plants. If we destroy their habitats, we will lose them forever.

Local Wildlife

What wildlife is at risk in your area? Your library is a good place to find out about animals that live nearby. Conservation groups may be trying to protect rare animals in your area, such as butterflies and frogs. You can help out by writing down where you saw these animals, and referring to a map if necessary.

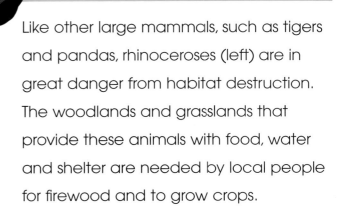

Like other large mammals, such as tigers and pandas, rhinoceroses (left) are in great danger from habitat destruction. The woodlands and grasslands that provide these animals with food, water and shelter are needed by local people for firewood and to grow crops.

WHAT CAN WE DO?

People who want to protect wildlife, are called "conservationists". Many have worked with governments to create wildlife parks in various parts of the world. These protect species whose natural habitat has vanished.

Other groups are working to stop pollution. New laws are also being made to help protect natural habitats from further damage.

Conservationists are working to protect the giant wilderness of Antarctica. This is cut off from the world by stormy oceans. A giant sheet of ice covers the land but there may be large stores of oil underground. Oil pollution could easily spoil Antarctica, but countries have so far worked together to protect this special habitat.

Many birds of prey (below) are endangered because of deforestation and other habitat destruction.

Groups like the World Wide Fund and Friends of the Earth are trying to save plants and animals by conserving habitats.

They also encourage governments around the world to ban the hunting of rare species, such as blue whales (right).

There are conservation projects to repair damaged habitats in many local areas (above). Clearing the rubbish from a pond, canal or riverbank can make a big difference to local wildlife. Creating a meadow area in a local park also creates a perfect habitat for rare wild flowers and insects, like butterflies.

Organic

Look out for vegetables and fruit in the shops with an "organic" label. This means this food is grown without the use of chemicals. Organic food takes more work – more weeding is done by hand instead of using sprays. But it does not harm wildlife, such as birds and butterflies, and it's better for you!

WILDLIFE GARDEN

You can help wildlife in your area by creating a wildlife garden at home or at school. You can also encourage wildlife by growing plants on a balcony or in a windowbox. Plants with strong colours and smells will attract butterflies and bees.

Insects attract animals that feed on them, such as spiders, birds and mice. You may even get a visit from a fox!

Spider on its web

Fox

Bird with worm

Create a Habitat

Here are other ways to make your garden into a nature garden:

- Wild grasses attract insects such as grasshoppers and provide shelter for mice and shrews.
- Create shady areas and sunny spots that will appeal to different animals.
- A pile of logs will attract beetles and woodlice, and the birds that eat them, such as wrens.
- Even a small pond will soon attract a large variety of insects and frogs.
- Bird feeders encourage birds into your garden.

Snail

Bee

LIVING WITH NATURE

Many people believe that the best way to protect wildlife is to change the way we live. For example, we need energy to cook, to heat our houses or to drive cars and trains. But the power stations and engines that create most of our energy also create the pollution that damages habitats. If we can learn to save energy or use cleaner supplies, such as wind farms, there would be less pollution to damage the wildlife around us.

URBAN • SAFARI

You don't have to live near a forest or by the seashore to go searching for wildlife. You will be amazed by the plants and animals in your town once you look. Areas such as cemeteries, hedgerows and riverbanks are good places to start exploring. Take a group of friends, but make sure an adult is with you. If you take a wildlife spotter book, it will be easier to learn the names of animals you discover.

We are all part of the natural world around us. Everything we do is linked to it in some way. For example, even if we live in a city, the pollution we cause affects habitats far from where we live.

Everyone can help to reduce pollution. We can buy products that are made from renewable resources. We can also make sure that the things we no longer need are recycled (below).

Go For It!

Simple things can make a difference to the environment, like clearing up the litter in a local park. Litter can kill wildlife and if you want to do something to help, talk to your friends and see if they want to join in. Why not design a poster? Make your message clear and choose a picture that helps to explain the problem.

Say RUBBISH to RUBBISH

Recycle is Best

USEFUL WORDS

biome – our planet can be divided into giant zones, called biomes, each with its own climate and ecosystems.

climate – the usual pattern of weather in a part of the world.

community – the group of plants and animals that live in a particular habitat.

conservation – protecting wildlife from damage.

deciduous – trees that have broad, flat leaves that fall off the branches in autumn.

deforestation – to clear a forest of trees.

ecosystem – all the living things in a habitat, and the way in which they work together.

environment – the surroundings of any living thing.

equator – an imaginary circle around the Earth, halfway between the North and South Poles.

global warming – an increase in the average temperature worldwide, believed to be caused by pollution.

habitat – a place where particular animals and plants live and grow.

organic – organic plants and animals are grown or reared without the use of chemicals, such as pesticides.

plankton – tiny and often microscopic groups of plants or animals that live in the sea.

pollute – to make something dirty with waste or chemicals.

recycling – to use a product over and over again.

species – a group of living things that are very similar to each other and can breed together.

tropical regions – the warmest parts of the world, found either side of the equator.

Find Out More

Books: Geography for Fun (Franklin Watts); Worldwise – Rainforest (Franklin Watts); What is a Biome? (Crabtree)

Websites: www.kidsdomain.com www.factmonster.com www.howstuffworks.com www.ecokids.ca

PREDATORS

There are skilful and deadly hunters (predators) in your area. A cat uses many of the hunting techniques used by its big cousins like lions and tigers – moving slowly and quietly, keeping its body low.

INDEX

Photocredits

Abbreviations: l-left, r-right, b-bottom, t-top, c-centre, m-middle

Front cover t, 3b, 4mr, 6tl, 11, 11mr, 13bl, 13bm, 14 both, 15tr, 17tl, 20tl, 23mrb, 26ml, 31br — Digital Stock. Front cover ml & bl, 7blb, 9mr, 18bl, 23bl, 26tr, 27ml — John Foxx Images. Front cover c, 4bl, 5ml, 5mr, 7tr, 8br, 9tr, 16br, 20-21, 24br, 25br, 26mr, 30tr — Stockbyte. Front cover br, 1, 9bm, 12br, 13tr, 16tl, 21tl, 22br, 23mrt, 27r, 28r, 29br, 31bl — Photodisc. Front cover inset, 10br, 17tr, 29bl, 30-31 — Comstock. Back cover, 4tl, 5tl, 11bm, 16-17, 16bl, 17bl, 18c, 22tl — Corel. 2-3 — Flat Earth. 7ml — Corbis Royalty Free. 7blt — Otto Rogge Photography. 7c, 7br, 8-9, 12-13, 19bl, 26-27, 27br — Flick Smith. 8tl, 16mr — PBD. 15br, 18-19, 23tl, 24bl — Corbis. 19tr — U. S Fish and Wildlife Service. 21bl — Jamie Hall/National Oceanic & Atmospheric Administration. 24-25 — Peter Clark, Tampa Baywatch/National Oceanic & Atmospheric Administration. 25tr — National Oceanic & Atmospheric Administration.